I0568249

SURVIVING A SILENCED HEARTBEAT

Annette Harris

Surviving a Silenced Heartbeat © 2022 by Annette Harris. All Rights Reserved.

All rights reserved. No part of this book may be reproduced in any form or by any electronic or mechanical means including information storage and retrieval systems, without permission in writing from the author. The only exception is by a reviewer, who may quote short excerpts in a review.

Scripture quotations marked NLT are taken from the *Holy Bible*, New Living Translation, copyright © 1996, 2004, 2015 by Tyndale House Foundation. Used by permission of Tyndale House Publishers, Inc., Carol Stream, Illinois 60188. All rights reserved.

Cover designed by Nskvsky

Printed in the United States of America
First Printing: August 2022
The Scribe Tribe Publishing Group

THE SCRIBE TRIBE
PUBLISHING GROUP

ISBN- 978-1-958436-11-0 (print)

ISBN - 978-1-958436-12-7 (ebook)

DEDICATION

This book is dedicated to the memory of my late brother, Darryl Derunte Gaston. Thirty-nine years ago on August, 19, 1983, our family lost a true treasure in a horrific way. My traumatic reactions in response to his death as a child made me realize that there are or will be other children who have or will experience similar reactions in these types of situations. It is important for them to know they are not alone. Darryl, your death has inspired me to step up and tell my story in order to help someone else to find their *heartbeat* again.

To my other *heartbeats*, my late parents, Mommy and Deddy, you meant the world to me! I will never forget how you always loved on me. I was the last product of the expression of your love for each other. **Mommy**, you were the epitome of strength and resilience; you were determined to take care of and provide for your family in spite of the tragedy that we faced. I can only imagine that there were many days and nights that you secretly cried after losing your only son, yet you smiled through it all. You took the word of God at face value and made it practical so that you could go on and live for yourself and for us.

Deddy, I remember the personal talks that you and I had as you shared your true feelings about losing your only male heir. It was sort of a therapy session for you (and for me), as you expressed your love for him and how proud you were of what he had accomplished when he was alive. The funny stories and memories that we had of Darryl is what carried us through that difficult time. Hindsight is 20/20 and I know you both had the thought that if you had done something differently then maybe he wouldn't have been taken from us. But mommy and deddy, I say that you both did a superb job raising and being there for us! The Lord could not have blessed us with a better set of parents who truly loved their children!

I always say about my two remaining sisters *(Lois and Kay)*, "We are all that we have left." Even though we are married with our own families, our sisterly bond continues! We strengthen each other as we laugh, cry and reminisce together. Have we always agreed with each other? No! But we have not allowed disagreements to separate us. Mother always taught us that we were not only siblings but each other's best friends. I have learned so much from both of you and it has molded and shaped me into the woman that I am today! I have and will always appreciate what I have in my sisters, which is genuine and continual love! That love binds us together and helps us to *#heal.*

This book is also dedicated to you, the reader. There are probably a few reasons why you have chosen to purchase and read this particular book, but we know that something drew you in. Death is inevitable, but it is not an easy subject to deal with or even discuss. I pray that the words of this book will grab you as you read with the intention of being *#healed.*

SPECIAL THANKS

Dear **God**, I thank you for **who** you are and **how** you are in my life! If it wasn't for your grace and mercy, I wouldn't exist. You have chosen me to write this book for such a time as this! I heard you speak over me telling me it's time to share my story and I was obedient and stepped out on faith to accomplish it. Was it easy? Sometimes, yes and sometimes no, but I held on to You. You have given me the title, every word to type and every resource to reference. As was prophesied to me in 2021, God, you told me that you were going to give me the strategy to minister. Once I stepped out to do this work (which was an element of faith), it was going to seem like I was stepping on nothing but You would literally form the ground under my feet! You said that You 'got me'! And my God, You don't, You didn't, and You cannot lie!

Anthony, my husband, my prayer warrior, my support – thank you for standing in the background, exhibiting your strength while carrying me. From the time that I began writing this book and revisiting the trauma, you undergirded and covered me! If it wasn't for you asking the question of whether I needed to seek professional counseling/therapy during this process, I probably would have just cried through this project or maybe not have finished it. Thank you for observing me and seeing what I needed in order to complete what God has given me to do. When it comes to my projects and my goals, you always just ask one question, "Did you pray about it?" You have never stood IN my way, but BY me, while leading the way! I love you ALWAYS.

I am grateful for both of my sister's spouses, **M. Anthony and Keith!** I have never considered you as "in-laws" but my brothers! You play such integral roles in our family! Thank you for being so encouraging and only wanting the best for me!

To my nieces, nephews and grandnieces **(Darryl, Elaine, Demetrious, Kilan, Genell, Eliana and Mary-Ana),** although I haven't been blessed to bring forth children, I love each of you as if you were my own. Your laughter, smile and zest for life encourages me to endeavor to be the best auntie that you deserve! I am so blessed to have you in my life!

Apostle Deon (my co-host and dear friend), I must thank you for allowing the Lord to use you to prophesy God's word and instruction to me! There are many false prophets out in the world, but you sir are NOT one of them!

Felicia Dobie-Williams, you are a God-send! Who knew years ago when you were the resident therapist on my radio show, "Mind, Body and Soul w/ANet," that you would become my personal therapist! Thank you for taking me on as a client and for helping me to peel back the layers of hurt enabling my own *#healing* to continue.

Anthony, Apostle Deon Hunt, Felicia Dobie-Williams and **Adell DuBose**, thanks for taking time out to look at my collection of thoughts! Your varied feedback was so valuable!

Pastor Kevin McGee, I reached out to you in February and asked if you could take my own words and place them into poetry form and you did it within a matter of hours. I can't express my appreciation for you. Out of all the poems you've written for me and my show, "Heartbeat" is my absolute favorite as it was created to help me tell my personal story in order to find *#otherheartbeats*.

Brandie McCord, when I first learned of your many abilities, I was told, "Everyone needs a *Brandie*, but don't take mine, get your own!" Years later when I needed my own *Brandie,* I am so glad that you responded with enthusiasm to be my promotional assistant and professional photographer! We've been rocking and rolling ever since! I thank God for you and your phenomenal expertise, especially in this latest project!

Robert L. Gill I, you have been a consistent supporter of my projects (from broadcasts to podcasts to writing books) from day one! When it was time to establish my corporation, GetcaughtinANet Inc. I was glad to make you a part of this organization. Your encouragement has made the difference in staying back or moving forward. I thank God for you and your commitment to motivating others!

Scribe Tribe Publishing and Kristen R. Harris, whew! Words cannot express the way I feel about this collaboration! Kristen, I reached out to you years ago to interview you about your book, *God Put Me Up on Game*! That went well and then I interviewed (then) 10-year-old Jenysys about her book, *Think is a Powerful Word*! Needless to say, I was very impressed with your work, your zeal and your drive. Down through the years, many publishers have been knocking down my (email) door, trying to get my business. But when it came time to write my book, I prayed and asked God for His direction and I know He led me to you. Thank you for accepting me into "The Scribe Tribe Virtual Writers Retreat" and then taking me on as a client. Kristen, indeed you are a praying woman who is led by the Spirit and you move in excellence when it comes to your publishing company! Many thanks to you and your entire staff for helping to make my dreams come true as a first-time author!

Table of Contents

FOREWORD

G rief is overwhelming and can be considered one of the most painful experiences any human will ever encounter. Losing a loved one can trigger a myriad of emotions that can reduce an individual's ability to cope with and understand what has occurred. When a loved one dies suddenly or tragically, the family is left to deal with the trauma of how they died.

In my work as a licensed clinical professional counselor, I have treated multiple patients for grief related issues. Some have struggled with prolonged grief and even posttraumatic stress disorder (PTSD) in response to their loss. Although grieving is a normal part of loss, not everyone grieves the same. Children respond to grief differently from adults. While adults are likely to express their grief to a close friend or relative, children may find it difficult to speak or they may not react very much at all. The way a child grieves depends on their age and understanding of death as well as their ability to talk about their thoughts and feelings.

This book, *Surviving a Silenced Heartbeat*, addresses grief while also providing resources to the reader. I met the author, Annette Harris, 7 years ago while being a guest on her radio talk show entitled "Mind Body and Soul w/ANet." This is a show where she uses her platform to promote mental health awareness. Since meeting, Annette and I have stayed in touch and have consulted with one another on issues related to mental health.

In her book, Annette shares a compelling account of her own personal encounter with grief due to a sudden and tragic loss. Annette is no stranger to loss nor the emotional struggles that follow. Her book isn't just written from her own personal experience, but also from the heart and wisdom of a degreed psychology major. With her Bachelor's in psychology, Annette presides over the bereavement committee at her church. In this role, she works directly with families that are in pain due to the loss of a loved one. Annette brings comfort and offers genuine and gentle care to the families she serves.

This book deals with a very related topic that many people have faced or are facing. The author allows herself to be transparent and vulnerable as she shares her grief experience. Her book can help others understand grief from the perspective of a child as well as an adult. Just as in her church ministry, Annette's book serves as a comfort and a guide, in that she provides multiple resources for her readers and lets them know they are not alone.

Felicia I Williams, NCC, LCPC

Owner/Clinical Counselor at Agape Counseling Services, PC

PREFACE

#2022istheyearofHealing, is my God-given hashtag and inspired theme of this year! By the time you finish reading this book, it will be your hashtag and theme too!

One may ask, why are you just now writing about the impact of a tragic event thirty-nine years later? Well, it is very simple; I have never been impressed to write about it until now. Also, I want to share my personal story in order to heal others.

> *39 years*
> *And I still hear your heart beating*
> *As if it were only yesterday*

No matter how long it has been since you lost a loved one, the process of healing needs to take place. Everyone, and I do mean "every" person, will take death differently. Sometimes it helps to hear about the journey of someone else.

The personal experiences within this book were written from my eyes as a child. I wanted to be as transparent as I could so that my story could be relatable. You will experience some highs and lows, along with laughter and tears. You will also see that I have nicknames for certain family members, such as our dad. Wherever you see the name, "deddy", it replaces "daddy." Don't worry, that is what we called him; I did not misspell it!

If we are honest with ourselves, no one likes to go through the lows of this life alone. Being able to relate to others will help us to understand their pain. This will in turn help to facilitate mental, emotional and spiritual healing for all.

#2022istheyearofhealing

Heartbeat

The sound of life
Yet sometimes
The heartbeat can be heard
After life is gone
39 years
And I still hear your heart beating
As if it were only yesterday
The way we were as children
Playing
Going to school
Going to church
living life
I hear the heartbeat
Living in a time
Where all we had were each other
Sisters and one brother
A family of love
That never failed
Even though we experienced
A portion of our love language
Separating no longer bound in wedlock
I could still hear the heartbeat
You see love is a powerful thing
And when you are surrounded
By so much of it

You can't help but be glad
When you should be sad
Because you can still hear
The heartbeat
Growing up wasn't always easy
But momma
Taught us that our strength
Was bound up in the heartbeat
God whose heart beats the greatest
Gave us his greatest heartbeat
And that heartbeat
Made our hearts beat
And so, we lived our young lives
Enjoying the Love
That emanated from the heart
But what happens
When that heartbeat
Goes silent
When that heartbeat can no longer be heard
When we're no longer sisters and one brother
But only sisters
That's when my heart stopped beating
That's when I became the walking dead
Living but not living
Trapped in grief
Mad at heaven, the earth, and hell
Because someone stopped
Your heart from beating
Couldn't comprehend
Why this was allowed
Because not only did you die

But a part of all of us died
The connection
Was severed
And I couldn't hear the heartbeat
Blaming myself
Wondering if I could have done something
Maybe I could have mimicked Joseph
And told my dream
Then it would not have become reality
And perhaps I could still hear the heartbeat
Grief told me I was guilty
And when I was at the point
Of giving in completely
I heard a heartbeat
I immediately thought it was my own
And I wondered how could
my heart sound so loud
But I realized
It wasn't mine
It was yours
You see I allowed misery and grief
To mute your heartbeat
I didn't understand that your heartbeat
Never stopped
But it
Was contained in
every memory
Every thought
Every image of you
It was then that I was made whole
Mind Body and Soul

Because what I thought was lost
Was now found
God allowed me to hear
Your heartbeat
So that I can help others to hear
Heartbeats
Those who are bound in misery and sadness
There are so many heartbeats
yet to be heard
And even as I read this
I can't help but smile
I can't help but to look out in the audience
And see you smiling back at me
Because right now
I hear your heartbeat
Composed by: Pastor Kevin McGee

PART 1 – MY PERSONAL EXPERIENCE

CHAPTER 1

In The Beginning was a Heartbeat

Let me create a scenario for you about my *heartbeat...*

The way we were as children
Playing
Going to school
Going to church
living life
I hear the heartbeat

My family is very important to me. Everything that concerns them, concerns me. When they hurt, I hurt and when they are happy, I am happy. When I was a child, I always prayed that death would NOT meet me or my family members. It was a naïve prayer but one that helped my young mind to make it through life. My immediate family, which consisted of my parents and siblings, was so close that I could not bear the thought of losing any of them to death.

I am the youngest child of five siblings. When I arrived on the scene, there were two sisters and one brother, Darryl, ready to welcome me. Unfortunately, another sister, who would've been the second child born to my parents, did not survive after living on earth for only a few short months. *I have often wondered if I would have been born if she lived.*

This is our birth order: the oldest sister is four years older than our brother and our brother is two years older than the middle sister and I am two years younger than that sister. Yes, they saved the best for last! So technically, when my parents began having children, they had one every two years, including our sibling that passed away.

As the story goes, one of my sisters, who is a little over two years older than me, was not initially happy about my arrival at all! If she could have had her way, she would have arranged for me to be taken back to wherever I had come from. In fact, when I became older, she shared with me her true feelings; she did not want me there at all! In her defense, she was the baby of the family for two years and seven months before I came along to take away the "baby" crown! The nerve of me!

Being the youngest meant that I had to accept what I was born into. I did not have my choice of family, siblings–in fact, who does? I really hated being called the "baby" of the family because I did not want to be treated like the baby. I wanted to be grown and older like my siblings. But truth be told, sometimes I wanted to be babied and nurtured. After a while, I adjusted into allowing my siblings to look after me and take up for me.

My sister (the same one who did not want me around when I was born), always bragged about how she would fight off the young boys who would taunt and tease me in school. There were quite a few young boys who really liked me but they did not know how to show it or express themselves properly. Instead of just walking up to me and telling me that they liked me, they would make fun of me. Then there were the times when the young girls who were jealous of me would try to start fights with me.

They did not stand a chance in carrying out any of their attacks against me because my sister was definitely not having it! She took great pride back then in standing up to protect me. I definitely appreciated the protection, but the catch 22 was that I knew I would be teased by my peers for not taking up for myself. I was never one to run toward confrontation; I always shied away from it. But my sister obviously got over not wanting me around and took it upon herself to defend me! Looking back on it all, I appreciate her efforts because it showed her sincere love for me. She has always said that she was the only one who was ever allowed to tease me and no one else! All kidding aside, both of my sisters and I have a great relationship with each other.

Once, I remember being taught how to fight by my brother and our father. It may have been a situation where I was being bullied, although I do not quite remember what brought it on.

I was in my bedroom that I shared with my mother (my parents were divorced by this time). Our room was the master bedroom, which faced the front of the house. It had two walk-in closets on either side of the room and it was pretty spacious. I was standing in an open space near one of the walk-in closets and that is where my boxing lesson began.

Both my dad and brother said to me, "Show us how you fight." Well, I closed my eyes and started swinging my arms wildly in the air as fast and hard as I could. When I stopped, I thought that I had really done something! They both looked at me and started laughing so hard! They told me that if that was how I was going to fight then I was going to get creamed and lose every time! When they stopped laughing, we got down to business.

Our father, who was a professional boxer, took the lead. Dad assumed the boxing stance and said to me, "Baby girl, this is how you must position yourself to fight." You need to keep your eye on your target and guard yourself at all times. Then he showed me how to strike and land punches.

I had no doubt that *deddy* obviously had taken time to show Darryl these techniques because he was showing off his boxing moves too! I was impressed by watching them both and I did exactly what they told me to do! I was fighting and defending myself so well that they both said, "Okay, okay, you got it now, you can stop!"

It is safe to say that on that day, I found out the proper way to fight!

Living in a time
Where all we had were each other
Sisters and one brother
A family of love
That never failed

My parents were on the verge of divorce, and I was only on the earth a few years by the time it was official. However, I can remember early on in my life sitting down for dinner with the whole family. We enjoyed happy times together as one family unit.

I come from a family of singers and preachers on my mother's side. My mother and her siblings even established their own gospel singing group called the *Adams' Sisters* when they were young. My uncles, their brothers, would play the music for them on the organ, piano, and guitar. They sang everywhere, at concerts, church services, special gospel events, you name it! During that time, they were popular and could be compared to certain gospel singing groups such as the Clara Ward singers, the Davis Sisters or the Barrett Sisters of Chicago, Illinois. Of course, singing became a part of our lives. Oh yeah, we had it honestly! As children (and even to this day), we could make up a song about literally anything.

My brother would create songs out of thin air. Once while my family was sitting down to eat dinner, my sister noticed that some particle was floating in her pop, and she exclaimed, "There's something in my pop!" My brother belted out a tune and added the simple lyrics, "There's something in my pop, something in my pop!" And wouldn't you know it, we all joined in and started singing this new "song" with him! Then we would all burst into laughter! Those were the best of times! It was a time when life was carefree and I was able to enjoy being nurtured and raised by our parents and growing up with my siblings. This family time together allowed me to interact with each *heartbeat*, and I absolutely loved every minute of it!

Darryl, was always the jokester of the family, yet he was sincere, sweet, caring and protective of his sisters and of our mommy. He assumed the role as the man of the house, when *deddy* physically left and moved out. As the only male in the house, you had better believe that he took this responsibility seriously!

Mommy had full custody of all four of the children, and *deddy* had certain weekends with us. My mother was not the type of person that would purposely keep us away from our father. So, on his court appointed weekends, we went to stay with our dad.

When our dad moved out of our home, he went to stay with his brother and family. Needless to say, it was a little crowded there, but we were young and small so we tried to make the best of our short weekend stays. Honestly, I never minded visiting with my dad, but I could not wait to get back home to mommy and my own bed!

Dad would take us out to work with him on the weekends. At that time, my dad owned a food truck and he would sell food to companies on their breakfast, lunch and dinner breaks. Do not get it twisted, food trucks were very popular back in the 1960s and 1970s; they did not just recently come into existence!

We had a Saturday morning routine. We would get up early to watch him prepare the food. He made breakfast sandwiches, some with cheese eggs (my dad made the best cheese eggs this side of heaven), crispy bacon, tasty sausage and other breakfast items. There were many times that we would help him to cook and package the food items. From there, we would load up the truck with the food and all four of us would pile in the front cab of the truck with our father. Off we would go to sell this delicious food! Sometimes deddy would allow us to eat the food as well because we were hungry too! We reaped the benefits of being his helpers!

Thinking back on these experiences, we may have been cramped in the front cab of that truck but we were family! We were together and at that point, that is all that mattered.

Whenever we would arrive at one of the destinations to sell the food so many people would come out of their jobs to purchase something to eat. They were overnight factory workers or those who worked various shifts and they would be so happy to see my dad and his food truck! Whenever they would see us hanging with him, they were very nice to us and would ask my dad, "Are these your children?" Of course, with a beam of joy, dad would reply "Yes," as he introduced us.

Because my dad had already been doing this for years, many knew him by name. But it was the first time I heard them call him by a name I was not familiar with. They would call him "Larry" or "Lorenzo," and I always wondered why because that was not his birth name. I later found out it was a nickname he had been given. This nickname was also displayed on the name tag of deddy's work shirt.

Even though we experienced
A portion of our love language
Separating no longer bound in wedlock
I could still hear the heartbeat

With the divorce of my parents came shame. During the 1960s, divorce was not common or looked upon favorably. If a husband and wife were to end their marriage, either party or both parties were looked at as "failures," and they had to answer to their extended family and society. Because of this misplaced shame, the children (the products of this failed marriage) felt the shame as well. I was hurt that our parents did not stay married and was also made to feel like there had to be something wrong with them and us. I did not understand at the time that sometimes two people cannot continue to be together because of their differences and that does not make them a failure. At that point, the *heartbeat* of our family just took on a different rhythm.

Unfortunately, somewhere along the line, as a child, I became more ashamed of our family's situation because no one else in our immediate family was divorced nor was their family busted up with one parent living in one place and the other parent living in a different location. The Gaston family, created by our mom and dad, became some sort of an anomaly.

When dad came around our house to visit us while driving in his food truck or his taxicab, that shame grew. I did not want anyone to see me with him or even talking to him. Sometimes my siblings felt the same way. I did not realize then that my dad was a serial entrepreneur! My father was a hard worker all of his life and that was nothing to be ashamed of! Our dad was showing us what it meant to work hard to get what you wanted in life.

Growing up wasn't always easy
But momma
Taught us that our strength
Was bound up in the heartbeat
God whose heart beats the greatest
Gave us his greatest heartbeat
And that heartbeat
Made our hearts beat

My mommy will always be the Greatest of All Time [*G.O.A.T.*] in my eyes! A gorgeous woman of God who was so intelligent, wise beyond her years, had many suitors to choose from, an awesome and powerful singer, the consummate professional as a beautician. (That was the best career to have with three daughters that had heads full of hair!) She was the owner of her own beauty hair salon with clientele of all races. Mama could lay any head of hair out! Now, that's beautician talk!

Our mother was determined to raise us in the way of the Lord. She had always been independent and once her marriage ran out of gas, she had the strength and guts to end it to maintain a healthy lifestyle for herself and her children. Mommy purchased a beautiful home in a well-manicured, upscale neighborhood. We had 3 bedrooms, 2 bathrooms, a dining room, living room, kitchen and a full basement that was revamped into her in-home hair salon with a separate entrance for her customers.

In our new home she continued to teach us to love one another and stay close to each other. We were all we had. We were blood. We were family. We needed to continue to hear the *heartbeat.*

When we first moved to the neighborhood, we were the first Black family on the block. Back then, the current homeowners were white and middle-aged. It was not until a few years later, that the area started to become more integrated because of the mass exodus of those white families. I was too young to understand the racial undertones and the *real* meaning behind that *exodus.*

The block we lived on was actually in between two of my aunts, my mother's sisters. One aunt lived one block to the east of us and the other aunt lived one block to the west. When I was younger, I always thought that it was a pretty sweet deal to be able to live close to our extended family.

Once the neighborhood became integrated, my siblings and I were able to make friends with the children of the new families! There was one particular family that lived at the beginning of the block that had as many children as our family, and we matched in ages and gender! So that meant that each of us had our own friend that was our same age to play with.

We would go outside, jump rope, play hide-and-go-seek, run around, hang out, you name it! But it was all good clean fun! Once the street lights came on, we had to be inside our house or there would be repercussions to pay! We could not bargain our way to stay out later because mother was serious about her rules. As children, we may have thought she was a little extreme in keeping tabs on us, but as adults we realize that it was for our own benefit. Mother was determined to have her children become productive citizens of society through her own form of discipline.

CHAPTER 2

The Development of the Heartbeat

And so, we lived our young lives
Enjoying the Love
That emanated from the heart

Because my siblings and I were raised in the church, the church was obviously *in* us. We would perform gospel concerts in our backyard and invite the neighborhood to come and listen. We even encouraged our friends to be a part of the choir and sing with us, and they gladly joined in! My brother had a bass guitar that he would play and we would sing and have "church!" I think my brother doubled as the preacher as well! We were not ashamed of our church upbringing and we wanted to spread the word of Jesus Christ to anyone who would listen. Years later, our friends and neighbors expressed how those backyard church services and concerts made a great impact on them and changed their lives for the better.

My mother never stopped us from having "church" in the backyard; I believe she may have been proud and saw it as our tool of witnessing about Christ. The word of God tells us that we should train and teach our children the way of the Lord and they will remember it once they are older. "Direct your children onto the right path, and when they are older, they will not leave it." **Proverbs 22:6 NLT**

This was definitely the truth in our case because our mom taught and directed us onto the right path, and we did not throw it away or disregard it once we became older. The evidence of this was the fact that we had never been to jail, never took or sold drugs, we never drank alcohol, we did not get involved with the wrong crowd or was at the wrong place at the wrong time, we did not hang out in the nightclubs, we did not engage in illicit sexual activity and the list goes on. Honestly, I never had the desire to do any of those things. Furthermore, I was too scared about what would happen to me if I ever did, not to mention receiving the wrath of my mother's hands!

As mentioned before, Darryl assumed the position as the male head of the house since my dad was no longer in the home. This is a responsibility that he felt was necessary to take on, not one that he was made to accept. He was very protective of his mother and sisters. He did not want us to be taken advantage of and did what he could do to prevent it.

Our oldest sister and Darryl were close in age, and they had a very close sibling relationship. They were each other's best friends. He talked to her about everything and vice-versa. After grade school, all three of my older siblings attended the same high school. I, however, never attended the same high school because by the time I graduated from eighth grade, we moved to a different city.

High school was an exciting time for my brother to shine, and shine he did! He found out who he was and what his purpose in life was to be. Darryl became a member of the speech team and drama club. He was excellent at both, winning awards while competing in speech tournaments. The drama club is where his acting career started.

I remember him being cast as the Black Count Dracula and he nailed that role! Our family and his friends all made sure to support him by going to watch his play when it was being performed at the high school. He was so excited about it and we were too! As I watched the entire play and saw how he moved across that stage, repeating his lines with great finesse, I thought to myself, "Wow, he is really good!"

Darryl brought that character to life in so many ways and I was very proud and impressed by what I saw! The only thing that grabbed at my heart and made me feel some type of way was when his character had to be placed in a big ole coffin at the end of the play. I knew it was just acting but there was something about that scene that did not sit right with me. It actually made me sad to the point of tears. Suffice it to say, that scene made me think of how it would be to lose my brother to death, and I hated that feeling! I was just glad that it was not real and that he was coming home with us after the play was over.

During his high school years, Darryl also found his voice as a radio broadcaster. When my brother began to mature and get older, his voice did too. When he talked, his words flowed like butter and he was smooth with his conversation. He did not waste his words and was intentional about what he spoke. The volume of his voice was so deep that he was labeled "the short man with the big voice." My brother's height was maybe between 5'5" and 5'7", but his voice was over 6' tall!

Our brother became the voice behind the morning announcements at school. Obviously, the administrators at that time felt that his voice and persona would work best to grab the attention of the student body. So, in the mornings, when students and educators assembled for their classes, the entire school could be assured to hear Darryl's smooth voice as he vocalized the school announcements for that day. I believe this is what started his interest in broadcasting.

Have you ever heard of Barry White? I could actually compare Darryl's voice to his to help you understand how deep the sound of his voice was.

My brother was not a popular sports jock, but that did not mean that he was not well known. In fact, his love of the arts was an example to others that a sports career was not the only way to express one's self or to display their talents. Honestly, I believe that hearing my brother's deep voice every school morning is what attracted so many to him. Many of the females wanted to date him and the males wanted to be like him. He was a great role model.

Because we were 4 years apart, my brother and I graduated in the same year of 1981. When he was graduating from high school, I was graduating from 8th grade. Yes, my mom had to fund two graduations in the same year!

I remember being emotional at my graduation because I had learned that our family would be moving to a different town, and I knew I would not get a chance to see my friends that I grew up with anymore since we would be at different high schools.

My brother's graduation was a little different. Darryl was becoming an adult and therefore, he was excited about the next steps in his life. He was able to celebrate with his friends and dwell on the accomplishments from high school. I recall everyone wanting to take a picture with Darryl after the graduation was over. There were so many pictures with female friends (these were probably the ones who wanted to be his girlfriend), other pictures were with his best friends, his former teachers/educators, etc. Many simply wanted to capture any last moments with him that they could possibly get. My brother was indeed popular!

I had always been so proud of my big brother and I saw so much potential in him. I really felt that he was going to do something with that larger than life voice along with his gifts and talents to positively change the world. I will admit, because he was our only brother, my sisters and I were very protective of him. Don't get me wrong, he was a real man and stood up for himself, but he knew that his three sisters always had his back, no matter what!

Darryl was determined to help mom in every way possible, and one of the ways he did that was to get a job to help with the finances at home. He found a job working at a restaurant, cooking and bussing tables. It was not beneath him to take on a job of this nature. He wanted to pull his weight so he could take the stress off of our mother. At that job, he endured racism, threats to his life and his body, all because of the color of his skin. As a black man, he endured it and continued working there for years because it was bringing in some financial relief.

There was one time in particular when Darryl had been threatened to be beaten up by a group of white boys. You want to know why? Because he was working while black. They had planned to jump him after work. If you knew our brother, you would know that he was not a violent person at all and would rather find peace in a situation. However, when he found out about the plan, he knew he had to take action to protect himself.

Now this was in the late 70s, early 80s, so a gun was not the weapon of choice like it is today. Typically, fights back then were handled by hands only. My brother called for backup from my older cousins and maybe their friends too. They were ready to fight for my brother! Trust me, when I tell you that they came in deep with their bats and anything else they could use to defend my brother and themselves, of course. The group of white guys thought they were ready but when they saw the backup my brother had and what they possibly could do to them, they backed off. I don't remember them ever bothering Darryl again!

As my brother continued his journey into adulthood, after his high school graduation, he began laying out his life's plan and goals. He continued working his job at the restaurant and began taking college classes. At the time, we lived in the southern suburbs of Chicago, Illinois. Darryl enrolled at Columbia College of Broadcasting in downtown Chicago, and he absolutely loved it! Now, this meant that he had to take public transportation to get back and forth from home to school. We only had one vehicle in the household and mom, of course, had to use her car to go to work. Because we grew up in the suburbs, going downtown Chicago seemed so foreign to me. Yes, I was a little sheltered!

My brother used to always try to teach my sisters and I practical things that pertained to life. One day, he took us on a bus ride to show us how to ride the bus and how to transfer from one bus to another so that we could successfully get to our destination. I was so nervous and a little timid because it was my first time. I recall him laughing at my reaction, but his reassurance calmed me down so that I could learn. Darryl did not want us caught off guard and wanted us to know what to expect, in case we had to travel without him. That was the love of a real brother. Obviously, I appreciated it because I remember that story over forty years later!

A short time after he started college, our uncle gifted Darryl with a car. The car was not brand new as it had been our uncle's car for years. If you knew anything about my uncle, you would know that he was particular about making sure his vehicles were kept in decent shape. So even though the car was considered a hand-me-down, it looked and rode very well! The car was a burgundy and cream Pontiac Bonneville, perfect for a nineteen-year-old young man, And boy, did my brother love it! It was such a nice gesture of my uncle, and we all appreciated it. Our uncle loved my brother and wanted to make an investment in him because he saw that Darryl was going to places and make a huge difference in life!

After that, Darryl was grown for real! At that point, he was working, going to college and had his own ride! When he would take us places in his car, we felt a little sense of independence because mommy was not in the car with us. Now do not get me wrong, we did not ditch mommy, but if she was at work, Darryl was able to pick up the slack by driving his own vehicle.

He used to pick me up from my high school after classes. Darryl also made sure that I had a ride home from my summer job at my high school. Back then, you were considered big time if you were picked up and dropped off at school as opposed to riding the school bus. My brother had me spoiled and I loved every minute of it!

One thing about our brother and I have always known it to be true, he loved his mother and his sisters! Darryl knew how to treat us as young ladies. He would open the doors for us, pay for our meals, and always show his concern for our well-being. We were never disrespected by him, and he would not tolerate anyone, whether it was our boyfriends, or someone trying to get close to us to disrespect us either. And they all had to be vetted by him.

While in high school, my second oldest sister and I had many suitors, either from school or from church. Darryl's vetting process was his own and he was able to decipher which guys were no good for us. He also knew those who said they were just our "friend" and those who really wanted to be more than friends. I guess you could call it a male to male check. Because of the divorce of our parents and with our dad not being in our home anymore, we needed that. Darryl was also extremely protective of whoever wanted to date our mom as well. He made it known that you had to come through him!

He was the watchdog of the house. He took it so seriously that sometimes it would get on my nerves because he was messing up my vibe. Little did I know at the time that some of those vibes that I had were "off" and no good!

I recall one time during a very hot summer, Darryl was outside working on his car. I got dressed because I wanted to hang outside with him and enjoy the weather. Sounds innocent, right? When I came downstairs and went outside, my brother looked up at me and ordered me back into the house and demanded that I change clothes! I was angry at him and asked *why*? He stated that the shorts of my outfit were too short and that I needed to change immediately! Hey, I thought I was cute wearing what I had on but Darryl thought other guys would see that "cuteness" and try to take advantage of me. He was not going to have his little sister being gawked at and whispered about in a negative way. He knew I was innocent and he wanted to keep it like that. I eventually went back in the house and changed my clothes. I respected my brother even though I did not agree with him at that moment. I had a lot to learn about the world and how people think when they look at me.

Since my second oldest sister and I are close in age, we did a lot of the same things or as she says, "I follow in her footsteps." She was correct in some instances. When it came to dating, going to proms and school dances, we had to get permission from mom but I firmly believe my brother had a say in it as well. Maybe he suggested that we should not be out long or that we should double-date? I do not know, but I think he placed a bug in mommy's ear. For all I know, it could have been something that he told her! I certainly would not be surprised!

Darryl was excited for his sister's triumphs as well. Once, our middle sister was selected to participate in our local town's beauty pageant. She is smart, beautiful and a gifted singer and she won first place! Darryl could not attend the pageant with us because he was at work but when he returned home that evening and saw her award, he was so excited for her! His pride beamed through and could not wait to congratulate her on this wonderful accomplishment!

One thing our brother did was to make sure he still had a good relationship with our dad. Before our uncle gave Darryl his car, our dad would pick him up from work or school and bring him home. They had long talks together which established a good male bonding. I believe Darryl would keep our dad updated on our accomplishments as we were growing up and maturing.

Darryl was a true man of God! He loved the Lord with all his heart and did not want to disappoint Christ. He took his relationship with the Lord seriously and he was not ashamed to tell others about Jesus Christ. This is one of the biggest things that I admired about him! I was so impressed that someone so young could have such a zeal as a Christian. He did not care if he was teased about going to church and claiming that he was a Christian or a saint of God. In fact, he purposely made it known!

The area we lived in was not devoid of gang members and drug dealers coming into our neighborhood to look for or bring trouble. My brother was observant of this but it did not deter him from ministering to them. Sometimes I would look out the window and see my brother on the sidewalk witnessing to various groups of young men.

He was instilling in them that they did not have to live a life of violence, shame and disgrace but they could turn their lives around. If they would give their lives to Christ, they could make a new start.

There was no shame in my brother's game when it came to Jesus Christ! I believe my brother's strong relationship with Christ and his own charisma made him trustworthy. Our friends and neighbors all got along well with him. He was well respected in the community.

We grew up in a Christian home. As I mentioned earlier, my mom's family is full of preachers, pastors and gospel singers. We attended a local COGIC church and we would be in service all day on Sundays and weekday services. It seemed like it was everyday though! Regardless of how often we would attend and the length of time, we were definitely taught the fear of God and of His love for each of us. Being raised in church may have gotten us teased, but we learned how to love God and how to love and treat mankind. I believe it also prepared us for whatever life threw at us, good or bad.

In my childhood church, my siblings and I were active in the choir and various youth events. I always wanted to be a part of the youth choir ("bigger choir") during the time we attended, but I had to settle for the Sunshine Band (the choir for babies as I would call it). All of my siblings were a part of the "bigger" choir and yes, even though I was not old enough to join, I felt slighted. I lived through it though.

We developed long lasting relationships and friendships as well. During the summertime while we were still in grade school, mom enrolled us in a local Vacation Bible School (VBS). Even though she worked long hours to provide for us, she did not want us (and it certainly was not allowed either) to lay around and do nothing all summer. VBS afforded us the chance to continue learning about Christ and further develop our relationship with Him and mankind.

I believe I was about 10 or 11 years old when my family left my childhood church and we began attending a totally different church. (And no, I never got to become a member of "bigger choir" before we left. Oh well!)

Our new church was quite big, which I was actually kind of intimidated by with over 1K+ church membership. However, I quickly realized that the size of this church did not matter. My mother made the decision to switch churches for our spiritual health. It was there that I was able to mature spiritually. When we joined the new church, we joined into a new family! When I tell you that the love and care that people had for each other was genuine, believe it!

Our mother became a member of the main choir and our brother became a part of the youth ministry and the broadcast ministry. That is right, his second love, broadcasting. (God and his family were his first loves.)

Darryl was trained to work behind the scenes as a cameraman in this ministry and he enjoyed every moment of it. Oh, I forgot to mention that this new church was located in the city of Chicago, which meant we had to travel from the southern suburbs to attend church service. The broadcast ministry was responsible for airing live television broadcasts on Sunday evenings. So, a Sunday for us meant staying in the city all day. We would travel to church for the afternoon service, grab lunch in the church cafeteria or off campus, then attend the evening service. Darryl was one of the main cameramen that worked the evening broadcast service. There were at least three big cameras in that church that captured the entire service, from the choir singing, to the pastor preaching to audience reactions, etc. It was a huge change from our previous church. All of it was a great sight to behold and as a family, we felt right at home. It was not because we were a part of a church that was famous at the time or because we were on television weekly, but again, because of the genuine love we experienced as newcomers and the opportunity to advance our spiritual walk.

Darryl normally worked the camera on the north side of the church and we decided that we wanted to sit near him when he worked. We were able to enjoy the service, listen to the Word of God, and clearly from those seats we had a chance to be near him. (As you probably should be able to tell by now, we were a very close-knit family). So that seating area became our regular seating. On any given Sunday, when Darryl was working the camera (which seemed to be all the time), that's where you could find us. Notice I said sitting near him but not distracting him. My brother was so focused on his job that we would not dare try to distract him. I do not know that we could even if we tried. I believe that is why that ministry department relied on him so much because he was awesome and dedicated to what he did.

Darryl became a part of the four D's, when he became a part of the television broadcast ministry. The four Ds consisted of close friends of my brother who had similar interests. We called them the four Ds for the obvious reason that each of their first names began with a D. But they had much more in common than their same first name initials. Although my brother was the youngest of the four, there was a brotherly bond that was developed and it held strong throughout their lives. They shared the same interest of the television broadcast ministry and they all performed the role of cameraman at our church. This propelled a few of them to further develop their careers in broadcasting, photography, videography, etc.

The four Ds hung out as brothers and they became a part of each other's family. This was perfect for my brother because he had grown up in a house full of females, so this male bonding was needed! And in turn, our family gained 3 brothers. All four families shared a mutual bond and I still call them my brothers to this day. One thing that I can say with assurance, all four of these young men were respectful, well respected, upstanding citizens in the community. They were saved, young men who loved God and their family. They were very protective of their families and their accomplishments. There was never a hint of jealousy or sabotage in their friendship because they celebrated each other's achievements. If you saw one, you saw the other. But also, if you hurt one, you hurt the other.

While my brother was living his dream of working in the broadcasting industry at church, he still held down one job while in college.

Additionally, while in college, Darryl hosted his own radio broadcast. He was able to showcase his talent, expertise and that great voice over the airwaves of Chicago. He made a great impact while hosting and he loved every minute of it. His radio show would air on Sunday mornings; what a way to start off a week! To turn on the radio and hear the smooth voice of my brother was something to be proud of. We were all very proud of him and knew he would become a giant in that industry. Others thought so too! I did not know until after the fact that in his process of career job hunting that he had a very productive interview with a well-known radio and television station in Chicago, WBBM News Radio. They were very impressed with him and his interview and made the decision to hire him!

As a broadcast journalist, Darryl, along with at least two of his brother-friends {from the D's}, covered the 1983 Chicago Mayoral race. When the late Mayor Harold Washington became the first African-American mayor of Chicago, Darryl was amongst the many journalists to share and be a part of that historical moment. He was so excited to witness this unique individual step into this prominent political position to make a positive difference in our community.

While taking classes, Darryl felt the need to look for an additional job to make more money to help to pay for his college tuition. My brother was self-determined and would not wait for something to be handed to him. He also never wanted to place more financial strain on our mother so he did what he had to do.

He searched for another job and found one that was near our home. For me, the only drawback was that he worked the graveyard shift. His hours were either from 11pm or midnight to around 7 in the morning. His new job was a clerk at an all-night convenience store. The precaution set in place for his safety and protection was to have an unmarked local police car positioned across the street from the store.

He worked there for at least two weeks and things seemed to be going great. This second job was helping him to get a step closer to his financial goals.

In 1983, I had a dream of a church service being held at our new church. I did not think much of this dream at the time because it was our new church home, and it is where we attended church service.

In the dream, I remember that the entire church was packed to capacity. In this huge church service, people were seated. Even more were standing because they could not find a seat, and then there were people waiting to get in. I could not for the life of me figure out why it was so crowded and what made all these people come to my *new* church.

As if that was not weird enough, it became even more strange because I saw my uncles, aunts, my maternal grandparents all in attendance. This was strange because they were members of a totally different church and would not have been in our church service unless there was a compelling reason to be there.

I dismissed the dream once I woke up and went on about my day. I do not even remember sharing the dream with anyone. I did not understand it and I did not dwell on it anymore.

As I mentioned earlier, my mother was a hard worker. As an entrepreneur, she actually worked extra hard. Being a phenomenal beautician, she always had a huge clientele. Mother would work so hard that she rarely took a vacation or time off of work. As her children, we would often tease her about it.

Remember when we joined our new church, mommy became a part of the sanctuary choir? Well, because she had a strong alto voice, she was asked to sing lead on a number of choir songs. The pastor of the church would always say that my mother had such an anointed voice that she could 'sing the devil out of anyone and anything!' Now, that was a strong voice! Whenever the church would go on revival crusades, it was not out of the ordinary for our mother to be asked to sing lead soloist.

In August of 1983, our pastor, the main choir, and the church made plans to travel to Oklahoma for a revival crusade. My oldest sister and brother both made plans to put their funds together to pay for my mother to travel to Oklahoma with the church and the choir.

Their reasoning was because our mother was always working but she needed to do this to get away for a few days. Their plan did not come without resistance. My mother was adamant about not going, but we overruled her, and we threw in the fact that she did not have to worry about paying for it!

Sunday, August 14, 1983, was my brother's 20th birthday! This was the same day that the travel bus for the crusade revival was leaving. We all rode with our brother as we took mommy to the church with her luggage to board the travel bus.

Even as we said our goodbyes to mommy, she was still saying that she did not want to leave us. We assured her that we would be okay without her for a week and that she would have a great time. When the travel bus left, my three siblings and I returned home to start our week of school and work. We were excited that we were finally able to get mommy to go on a vacation!

My oldest sister was in charge of us while mommy was away. Both she and my brother were the siblings with jobs at the time. Darryl drove himself and went to work as usual on that night, August 18th , and my sisters and I were home alone.

In the early hours of August 19, 1983, my oldest sister received a phone call from the local hospital. They asked if she could come to the hospital because our brother had been *hurt*.

At that point, my sister called my aunt and uncle who did not live very far away. She asked them to come and take her to the hospital because she was told that Darryl had been hurt. She woke us to tell us what was happening. She had limited information on the condition of our brother but that she was going to go and check it out. My aunt came to pick her up and when she left, I went straight to my brother's room and sat in there for a long time. We did not know any details; I just sat there and prayed trying to convince myself that he would be alright! I tried to draw conclusions in my mind by thinking, *he must have had a minor injury, or why would the hospital say that he was hurt?*

Later on, my uncle came to pick up my sister and I. We drove back to their home. He did not talk much or even at all on that short car ride and I wondered what was going on. *Why was he picking us up? Where was my oldest sister? What was happening with my brother?* These questions and more were running rampant through my mind and it was getting so loud. *Why weren't we being told anything?!*

We arrived at my aunt and uncle's home and I only remember my mother's two brothers being there. They had us sit in the family room and one uncle said to the other, "Should we tell them?" I'm thinking to myself, *tell me what?! Somebody, say something!* Then the second uncle agreed it was time to tell us...

CHAPTER 3

The Heartbeat Goes Silent

But what happens
When that heartbeat
Goes silent

"Darryl is dead…"

Those three dark words should never have come together in one sentence.

The walls started closing in, it got harder for me to breathe. *What was this foreign language that he was saying? I see your mouth moving, but the words that are coming out are not connecting! My brother is what? No, he was just at work last night! Not my brother, our ONLY brother! Please, there must be some mistake!*

That news made me scream, cry and take off running! I had no clue where I was going but I needed to get out of there, far away from this news.

There we were, five days after Darryl turned 20 years old. Five days after mommy saw her only son for the last time, faced with the harsh reality that Darryl was gone forever.

I went through a myriad of emotions, too many to count. *How did this happen? Was anyone sure it was him? Maybe it was a mistake. This cannot be real!*

The story that we were given was that Darryl was working his overnight shift alone, and somewhere in the early hours of the morning, the store came under siege by two assailants. It was a senseless robbery. Darryl was informed that he shouldn't feel threatened while working because an unmarked police vehicle would be watching the whole time from across the street. The procedure was to ring the silent alarm to alert them. The button for the silent alarm was located under the counter somewhere near the cash register. When the perpetrators came in with guns and demanded the store's money, Darryl followed the procedure and pressed the silent alarm. Our understanding is that the gunman saw him press the alarm and that's when he was shot, leaving him for dead. Darryl was pronounced dead on arrival at the hospital. When my oldest sister received the call to come to the hospital because he had been hurt, he was already deceased. I realized later that whoever made the call was using wisdom in how they relayed the information. If they had told her over the phone that he was dead, they would not have known what her reaction would have been, and she needed to get to the hospital safely.

My other sister and I were still at the home of our uncle and aunt when our extended family began to arrive. I remember seeing my dad's brother walking around in the backyard in unbelief. My maternal grandmother arrived and she was taking it pretty hard.

My mother finally arrived after flying back from the revival crusade in Oklahoma. Of course, her vacation trip was cut short, but our church made arrangements to make sure she was able to catch a flight back home to be with her family.

My older sister was the one who phoned my mother and told her that Darryl died. My mother went into full denial mode and even said, "Who? Not my Darryl!" Mommy's constant rejection of going on that trip was even more founded; her spirit told her something was not right about leaving her children.

When reality began setting in for mommy, she went to her source of strength to make it through—she called on the name of the Lord! When she prayed, God heard her and helped her. Now, that does not mean that the devil was going to stop discouraging her or trying to take advantage of the situation because that is his M.O.

Mommy admitted that she was so hurt that when her flight took off, the devil tried to talk to her psyche and tell her that the plane was going to crash and she would die, just like her son! But the Spirit of God took center stage in her mind and heart and comforted her with the following words: "YOU will not get sick! YOU will not lose your mind! And, YOU will not die!"

Mommy took that and ran with it because that meant that God was going to see her through this. That confession was so strong for her that it became real for her remaining children and our extended family.

As a child, I was so glad when mommy came home, I just wanted to be in her arms so that she could assure me that everything would be alright.

My brother's death was considered a homicide and the assailants were on the run. They had also stolen my brother's personal belongings, including his wallet, which contained his identification with his address and his car that my uncle had just given him. Since they stole his personal items, we decided that it was not safe for us to return home to live. We did not know if the assailants would come after his family or not. For a while, we stayed with two of my mother's sisters and their families, until we eventually found another place to live safely.

Of course, after my brother's death, our family had to plan his funeral. I remember that we chose his favorite blue suit to bury him in. My brother was a very sharp dresser, and he kept his appearance up. Darryl made sure that he kept his hair cut and he was well groomed at all times. Even on his dress down or casual days, he was still sharp. He did not purchase cheap clothes; he kept his shoes shined and was very presentable wherever he went. You see, as a young black man in this society, there is a certain way that he had to present himself to be taken seriously. Darryl definitely showed the world that he was successful and on his way to the top!

That's when my heart stopped beating
That's when I became the walking dead
Living but not living
Trapped in grief

I felt like I was in a daze as we prepared for his funeral. One day we had to go to the local mall to purchase items to wear for the funeral. When we arrived and got out of the car to go into the store, I remember looking around as if it was my first time going to the mall. We had been to this same mall time and time again! Although everything was the same, everything looked so different and strange to me.

I guess I was looking at life with a different set of eyes. Eyes full of sadness, sorrow and fear. Eyes that would NEVER behold my brother's face on this side of heaven. Eyes whose lights had gone completely out. I was hurting so bad. I had to take myself out of my own body just to exist. In other words, I separated my mental state from my physical state in order to push on and live. I did all of that without realizing that it was what I was doing.

The time came for the funeral service to take place. We had to lay my brother to rest. It was decided to have the services at our new church, primarily because it was the last church where my brother was a church member.

The night of the funeral, a long black shiny limousine from the funeral home came to my aunt and uncle's home to pick us up. It seemed like it was the longest ride to get from the south suburbs to the south side of Chicago to the church, but we finally arrived.

Blaming myself
Wondering if I could have done something
Maybe I could have mimicked Joseph
And told my dream
Then it would not have become reality
And perhaps I could still hear the heartbeat

Do you remember the dream I had about the crowded church service? Well, let me refresh your memory. Prior to this tragedy, I dreamt that my family and I were attending a church service in the new church where my mom and siblings had joined as members.

There were a few of the strange things about the dream that stood out to me:

1) It was crowded and packed to capacity; every space in that 1,000+ seat auditorium was filled; it was standing room only with people still trying to get inside.

2) My extended family (including my maternal grandparents, aunts and uncles) was present for this service, even though they were church members elsewhere.

Yep, you got it. The church service that I dreamed of was my own brother's funeral! I literally dreamt about his funeral service before he even died. Now I didn't realize this until after my brother's funeral was over but it was a harsh reality to grasp.

My brother's young, 20-year-old life impacted so many people in such a positive way. There were so many people at his funeral that many could not get in! And that part in my dream where there was standing room only–I found out that people were lined up outside of the church, waiting to pay their last respects. Our extended family on both mommy's and deddy's side were there. This was an unbelievable tragedy to experience but we sure did receive so much love and support from everyone. Everyone was touched and hurt by the loss of Darryl.

I had an unusually hard time and I cried so much during the service that there are many things that I do not remember about the actual funeral service. I do recall that when they played a recording of my brother's voice, I lost it! It was a recording of his radio broadcast that he hosted. The short man with the BIG voice. His words belted out so strongly over the speakers that night that it seemed like he was there..alive..still with us!

Well, I think I must have cried out so loud because before I knew it, the nurses picked me up and took me out to get fresh air and water to help calm me down. I only reacted that way because I just wanted my brother back!

When our deddy went to view Darryl's body, he leaned over and kissed him on his forehead. I had never seen anyone do that to a dead body, but it was obviously his way of coping. Everyone displayed their own actions and reactions during the funeral to help them to get through it.

My uncle (my mother's brother who gave Darryl the car) had recently become a pastor. He got up to give words but I was so zoned out that I do not even remember everything he said. I was just so glad that he was there.

Another special individual who was grieving with us was my brother's girlfriend. They were in love with each other and Darryl was planning to marry her. He was very mature for his age and knew early what he wanted out of life. My heart always bled for her after his death, thinking of the life that they could have had together.

Our pastor at that time gave the eulogy. It was not easy for him either because he loved and respected my brother so much.

My brother always had a certain positive aura about himself that drew others to him. His smile was as big as the sun in that it would brighten up your day. If you had come into his presence with an issue or problem, he found a way to either help you resolve it, make you laugh about it, or encourage you to refocus so you could see that situation in a different light. He was contagious in the best way possible! He treated everyone with respect, especially his elders. Darryl treated others exactly how he wanted to be treated, as a human being, as one who had a chance to make something out of their life.

I know I just painted him as the poster child or the best human being to ever walk this earth but that description is obviously not wrong when over a thousand people showed up to pay their last respects at his funeral.

At some point during the funeral, our pastor went to pin my brother. Let me explain what I mean by *pin*. About eight months prior, on December 30, 1982, our pastor preached a sermon, entitled, "I Command You to Live!" The text was taken from Ezekiel 37:5, where it talks about the dry bones living again. It was such a comforting and encouraging message that could be taken in so that we all could live again in spite of what we are faced with. Whether it be sickness, turmoil, disappointment or even death, we could still LIVE!

That message became a movement all on its own! I believe it was a series of messages under that title and items were created with the word *LIVE* and the corresponding scripture on it. A lapel pin was also created and mass produced enabling many to purchase it not only to wear, but to apply the concept to their lives.

That lapel pin is what our pastor pinned Darryl's suit jacket with. It was such a powerful and meaningful moment. Although this action was of a metaphorical nature, our pastor was still commanding Darryl to LIVE!

You see, after death, there is definitely judgment! God is not the God of the dead but of the living! Unfortunately, we focus so much on this side of earth as if we are staying here forever. But death and the Resurrection are sure! So yes, Darryl will LIVE again!

It is important to note here that my sisters, mom and I adopted the word *LIVE* into our daily conversation. We replaced the word *bye* with the word *LIVE* whenever we left each other's presence, in person or on the phone.

CHAPTER 4
Minus One Heartbeat

When that heartbeat can no longer be heard
When we're no longer sisters and one brother
But only sisters

After the funeral, my mom, my sisters and I had to try to pick up the pieces and move forward in our lives. We had to learn to navigate through this new and different phase in our lives, but the question became, **how?** How do we adjust to this new normal? Life without Darryl was unbelievable. And 39 years later, for the most part, it still is.

I had so many questions! At 15 years old, I was the youngest and my mind was still maturing and developing. I thought that if I honored God by choosing to serve Him and live this Christian life, that He would protect me and my family, even from death.

How could something like this happen to a good Christian family?

We were brought up in church all of our lives. We went to church, what seemed like every single day; all day on Sundays, Tuesday night Bible study, Friday night worship service, not to mention annual revival services that would last weeks at a time! We attended church so much that it was like our extracurricular or recreational activity! Our friends would tease us so much because we were *always* in church! My mother took us to church and did not just drop us off there and leave us. She also instilled the word of God in us at home, by teaching us the difference between right and wrong. Someone may have labeled us as being sheltered, and there may have been some truth to that. The only time any of that bothered me was when my outside friends brought it to my attention. Otherwise, I was fine with how mommy raised us.

Our mother was determined to raise her children in holiness. Her efforts to make sure that we grew up in a positive environment was meant to nurture good character and yield productive, successful human beings. Our mother did not allow us to hang out with or spend the night with anyone, including family. Unfortunately, there were some in our extended family that were not practicing living the life of a Christian or a saint of God. Many were into that night life, which included going to bars, smoking, drinking alcohol, drug use, sexual promiscuity, and listening to "worldly" music (if it wasn't Gospel, it was worldly). In fact, one of our relatives owned a tavern in the city of Chicago. I only learned of that because I was never allowed to go (and rightfully so, I was just a kid).

Don't get me wrong, mommy wasn't only protective of us when it came to certain sides of the family. To a certain extent, she was protective of us with all family and close friends as well. In other words, as a divorced mother of four, she could not and would not let her guard down in raising us.

I only remember a few times in the summer, when mom allowed us to go and spend the night with our aunt, our dad's younger sister and her family. As a kid, those were the best of times! Whenever we would travel to their home, deddy would take us and we would be so excited. I can still remember the smell of potato chips wafting through the air as we passed by the old Jay Potato Chip Factory. Of course, deddy pointed it out to us because he loved showing and teaching us things. Whenever I smelled it, I just wanted to eat potato chips!

I also remember playing outside at dusk and after dark. My aunt and uncle had four children as well so we each had someone similar to our age that we could play with. I would look up at the sky and realize how beautiful it was when the sun went down. Why did it seem like the colors in the sky were more beautiful in the city than the suburbs? When the sun went down, it was a deep red orange and when it turned real dark; it was like a rich purplish blue. I laugh to myself now because I realize that the city sky may have looked different because mommy did not let us stay out after dark, and I did not see much of the night suburban sky!

In my aunt and uncle's home, they played different kinds of music. My cousin loved the Isley Brothers, so that's what we listened to while there instead of gospel music. There were other groups, like Earth, Wind and Fire and maybe the Jackson 5. In my aunt's defense, I think I recall her playing gospel music from time to time. My aunt did respect what our mother was instilling in us as young Christians.

Why am I sharing all of this? Because we were known all over as a good Christian family that attended church; a family that loved and lived for God. So again, my young mind questioned, *"how could this happen to us?"*

Couldn't comprehend
Why this was allowed
Because not only did you die
But a part of all of us died

When I was much younger, my mother taught me how to pray. I came to understand how important prayer is. I would pray for everything, it seemed. Indeed, my family has always been at the top of my prayer list. One of the prayers that I would ask God for was to keep us from dying. I asked if He could allow us to live until He returned to rapture us all away together. That was my desire, it was an innocent prayer that I prayed every day. Honestly, I never wanted to experience losing a sibling or my parents; I always thought that it would be too much of a great loss for me to handle!

"Now I lay me down to sleep, I pray the Lord my soul to keep. If I should die before I awake, I pray the Lord my soul to take."

That was the introduction to my young prayer and then I would conclude with calling out the name of each family member, and I would ask the Lord to spare their lives and bless them. I would then go to bed and sleep peacefully. If there was ever a time that I had forgotten to pray those words, I would feel guilty or feel like something bad could happen to my family.

I have always believed in the power of prayer. Darryl's death was the first immediate family member to pass away. I must admit that I have often wondered, could I have done anything at all to prevent his death? Were my prayers not enough? Was God not listening to me when I asked him to spare my family from death? I was so hurt and confused.

My brother was an honorable, respectful young man who had only reached twenty years old. Why was *his* life cut short? Was this the plan all along, for him to only live to be twenty? It just did not seem fair. Should we look at a new life being born into this world as only temporary?

Darryl was a true man of God with so much potential and indeed had a lot of work left to do here on earth, but he was not afforded the opportunity to do it. I always admired how he carried himself and conducted business. Darryl showed me the great potential a young person could have. His hard work ethic as a young adult was passed on to me without me realizing it. I learned from him that if you are an honest human being and treat others right, God will reward you.

Be happy about it! Be very glad! For a great reward awaits you in heaven. And remember, the ancient prophets were persecuted in the same way. St. Matthew 5:12 NLT

My brother's death was classified as a homicide, so that meant that the perpetrators had to be caught, charged and brought to trial. This was the next worst thing that we had to deal with outside of his murder.

First of all, the assailants were teenagers, who were close to my age. These young boys were out in the wee hours of the morning performing a crime, when they should have been at home in the bed so they could be in school the next day! Secondly, it was suspected that they performed this horrible act as some sort of a gang initiation. Lastly, they were not caught right away, which is another reason why I could not trust people. In my mind, since we did not know who was responsible, everybody was a suspect to me!

In the fall of 1983, I returned to high school and found out that I was in the same homeroom class as the sibling of one of the offenders. I was devastated and it made me retreat more into the shell I was already in. It was so traumatic for me that I began to wonder if we were placed in the same classroom on purpose. I wondered how that could happen. I did not want to be anywhere near them or be associated with them, the pain was too great. I did not want anything or anyone to remind me of the devastation that my family and I had just experienced a month prior.

I did what I thought I could to cope. There were times that I felt like the entire school body was against me. I felt like they probably knew who murdered my brother, but they weren't forthcoming about what they knew. I started distrusting my friends. I didn't feel like they had my best interest at heart. I felt alone, while I was hurting deep inside. My grades began to decline because I wasn't able to focus. All I could think about was the fact that Darryl was gone forever. I was suffering big time.

I remember there were times that I would be sitting in class trying to listen to the teacher, and my mind would trail off. Without warning, the tears would overwhelm me, push past my eyelids and rush down my face like rivers of water! I literally had to get up and run out of the classroom because the thought of my brother no longer being alive was so fresh, unfair and unreal! I tried to compose myself with whatever I had within me, but it wasn't enough. Those outbursts were frequent enough that it became a common theme for me. I remember one dear friend of mine who told me that they felt so sorry for me and how I was trying to cope. They wanted to help but didn't know how and even likened my behavior and actions to a zombie. I was just a shell moving around like the walking dead.

I really believed at that time that absolutely NO ONE could be trusted except those who were related to me by blood. I began to live my life in fear. I was leery of anyone trying to get close to me or my family; I thought they were up to no good. Yes, I had a little paranoia going on. Paranoia is an unrealistic distrust of others or a feeling of being persecuted.

There was one time after we finally moved from the area where my brother was killed that this paranoia became real to me. We were invited to an outing with some of our church friends, and we were home getting ready. Well, we were supposed to be there at a certain time but we were running late. One of our dear friends called the house to check on us and to see if we had left yet. I answered the phone, "Hello?" The caller responded, "Y'all better get out of that house now!" My heart started beating so fast and I could not say a word or even respond. That caller scared the mess out of me, and I immediately hung up the phone. I really thought that we were going to be attacked! Or that we were being warned that someone was coming to kill us, like they killed Darryl!

Thankfully, it was a false alarm because it was only our friend being silly and just telling us to "get out of the house" at that moment because we were going to be late for the outing. Whew, Lord have mercy, because it sure sounded like a threat to me! Can you say, paranoia and PTSD? I was suffering from it badly.

Now you can understand how that distrust of others had me on a tailspin! Unfortunately, at that time I did not realize that this was happening to me. I just continued to function on a daily basis. Or so I thought...

Trust me, the mind is a very powerful tool. It can play tricks on you without your consent. This is a good time to stop and share my mantra: Everything starts in the mind!

We must guard our minds and not allow any and every thought to enter. You need a good security guard at the door of your mind, and I recommend the Holy Spirit.

"Then you will experience God's peace, which exceeds anything we can understand. His peace will guard your hearts and minds as you live in Christ Jesus." Philippians 4:7 NLT

Of course, when a horrible offense takes place, such as a murder, families should expect a trial to determine what price the offenders should pay. It is definitely not pleasurable for either party, but it must be done. I'm not sure exactly how long it took before the offenders were caught and charged with the death of my brother, but it seemed like it could not happen soon enough!

I went to court every day. The courtroom was packed on both sides of the room. It was standing room only, just like at my brother's funeral. Many people came to show support for us to see that justice was served. But there was also support for the offenders, who claimed they did not commit the crime. Of course, my family and I sat on the prosecution side of the gallery, and I made sure not to make eye contact with the other side. I was fearful and afraid of them. It was hard enough listening to testimony after testimony of what happened to my brother on that fateful night.

Day after day, we would have to get up, get dressed and be escorted to the courthouse for the events of the trial. Yes, I said *escorted*.

Whenever my family would enter the courtroom, we would be harassed and threatened by the offender's family and their supporters. They threatened us with bodily harm because they did not believe that their loved ones were guilty. The threats were so intense and believable that my family was assigned a police escort. We were taken in and out of the courtroom and courthouse privately and an officer was also assigned to protect our home, 24-7! We could not take their threats lightly because obviously, violence was how they solved their problems. I mean, look at the situation we were already dealing with!

I was grateful for the police escort. There was one particular police officer who became our guardian angel. He took his job very seriously in making sure that my mom, sisters and I were well taken care of. I cannot forget to mention that my brother's close friends and our family also were there to support us. They were present in court and one of the four D's made sure that he was there *every* single day! He said he wanted to make sure that whoever took away the life of his friend would be held accountable. There was so much love and support shown for my family that it helped us to push through that difficult phase of our lives.

When my mother was called to testify on behalf of my brother, the defense played dirty. They tried to distract her by showing her pictures of my brother's deceased body. I still cannot understand to this day why that was done, but it was definitely heartless and cruel. Why show a grieving mother a picture of her child lying face down dead in his own blood? What was that supposed to prove? All I know is that my mother showed immeasurable strength on the witness stand because, honestly, I do not think I could have handled it. We did what we could as family and friends to comfort her afterward.

Truthfully, I will never know how she sincerely felt or how she processed it. I really wish that my family and I had known enough about counseling and therapy back then to realize that it was okay to utilize it. We truly could have used additional guidance and or advice on how to handle the stages of grief after losing Darryl in such a tragic way. Sure, we were receiving spiritual support, individually and corporately, but therapy sessions would have no doubt allowed us to peel back the layers of hurt, pain, confusion, etc. to get us to a place of *#healing*.

CHAPTER 5

Forgiving A Misguided Heartbeat

Mad at heaven, the earth, and hell
Because someone stopped
Your heart from beating

You are probably wondering what was the result of the trial. Well, both offenders were convicted, the shooter and the accomplice, although their sentences were very light to me. It was almost as if the system did not care because it was a "black-on-black" crime. Nonetheless, they were going to pay for what they did to an upstanding citizen. They took down another brother, one who looks like them, one who never did any harm to them or their families, one who was making a positive difference in the world. And all for what? A few dollars they received from robbing the store? Was it even worth it?

As you can imagine, I experienced additional anger. Especially, after revisiting everything during the trial, yet realizing that my brother was never coming back. In addition to that, the offenders are still alive and only served short sentences for the murder of my loved one.

Do you want to know what happened to me in the midst of dealing with that anger and confusion?

The love of God happened to me!

Please allow me to explain.

Once the trial was complete and the sentencing was handed down, I heard the Holy Spirit of God speak to me and tell me to forgive them. I will admit that I did not readily accept it and felt like it had to be a mistake or a familiar spirit speaking to me.

Forgive? As in "pardon," "excuse," "let bygones be bygones"? And just 'who' am I supposed to "forgive"? Uhm, that does not make sense to me.

If I can be most transparent, I certainly did not do it right away. Honestly, I wanted to make sure that what I heard was actually from God. I also wanted to hold onto my anger!

For goodness' sake, my brother was gone, never to return to this earth again! He would never see me complete school, get my degree, fall in love, get married, have children and I would not be able to see him do the same!

FORGIVE THEM...

This directive came back to me again and again, even in my dreams.

Some Psychologists define 'forgive' as a "deliberate decision to release feelings of resentment or vengeance toward a person or group who has harmed you, regardless of whether they actually deserve your forgiveness." [1]

Furthermore, "Just as important as defining what forgiveness is, though, is understanding what forgiveness is not. Experts who study or teach forgiveness, make it clear that when you forgive, you do not gloss over or deny the seriousness of an offense against you. Forgiveness does not mean forgetting, nor does it mean condoning or excusing offenses. Though forgiveness can help repair a damaged relationship, it does not obligate you to reconcile with the person who harmed you, or release them from legal accountability.

Instead, forgiveness brings the forgiver peace of mind and frees him or her from corrosive anger. While there is some debate over whether true forgiveness requires positive feelings toward the offender, experts agree that it at least involves letting go of deeply held negative feelings. In that way, it empowers you to recognize the pain you suffered without letting that pain define you.. This way you can heal and move on with your life." [1]

So there I was at 15, almost 16 years old, being told that I needed to forgive. Let me tell you, the Holy Spirit has so much wisdom! I did not need to go to the perpetrators and tell them directly that I forgave them, but I could release them in my heart. The Spirit of God knew that I needed to do this in order to heal and move on with my life. Otherwise I would have been stuck back in 1983, in my feelings not being able to be used by God to help others, like you!

PART 2 – DEALING WITH GRIEF AND BEREAVEMENT

CHAPTER 6
Dealing with Grief

B y now, everyone understands that the entire world has been affected by, and technically, under siege due to the Coronavirus pandemic. Countless lives have been lost as a result of the virus {as of April, 2022, 506 million globally}.

According to an article in USA Today, as of February 2022, in excess of 5 million children worldwide have lost a parent or caregiver to COVID-19.[4] Some children have become orphans, many families have become single parent homes, children have lost close friends, teammates and classmates. But please keep in mind, Covid-19 is not the only reason children have lost a loved one to death!

Trauma and PTSD are also a part of the grieving process. "Approximately 6 of every 10 men and 5 of every 10 women experience at least one trauma in their lives. About 8 million adults have PTSD during a given year."[7]

I want to address this a little further. We will first take a look at the stages of grief and some facts and statistics related to children and their handling of grief and death.

Stages of Grief

The **five stages of grief** theory, was developed by psychiatrist Elisabeth Kübler-Ross which suggests that we all go through five distinct stages of grief after the loss of a loved one: denial, anger, bargaining, depression, and acceptance.[9]

- The first stage in this theory, **denial** helps us minimize the overwhelming pain of loss. As we process the reality of our loss, we are also trying to survive emotional pain. Denial is not only an attempt to pretend that the loss does not exist. We are also trying to absorb and understand what is happening.[8]

  > For me, I couldn't believe my brother was dead, I was in **full denial**. I mean I literally sat in his room after my oldest sister received the call that he was hurt, and tried to reassure myself that he would be okay. I think my spirit knew something serious had occurred, but I wouldn't let myself receive it. To minimize the thought of him being dead, I kept telling myself that maybe he just experienced a minor wound. It was my way of initially coping while trying to comprehend what was happening at the time.

- In the second stage, it is common to experience **anger** after the loss of a loved one. We are trying to adjust to a new reality and we are likely experiencing extreme emotional discomfort. There is so much to process that anger may feel like it allows us an emotional outlet. This can leave you feeling isolated in your experience and perceived as unapproachable by others in moments when we could benefit from comfort, connection, and reassurance.[8]

I had fear and torment. I was scared of humanity and **angry** that someone felt bold enough to take away someone else's life for a few dollars or whatever their reasons were. I was so mad that my brother would never experience life as a mature young man, as a professional, as a husband, or as a father. I hated the fact that my brother's life was no longer. Darryl would not be there to tease me or keep us laughing with his funny jokes or be involved in any part of my adult life. I have so much love for my family, and I never wanted them to be physically harmed in any way. If they fell down and scraped their knee or experienced a small injury, my heart would hurt for them. So, imagine how upset and confused I was when my brother lost his entire life to murder. During this stage, the only comfort I could have received was for my brother to be brought back to life. For years, I was also infuriated with the owner of the convenience store. I felt like they didn't protect my brother's life and placed him in harm's way.

- When coping with loss, in this third stage, it isn't unusual to feel so desperate that you are willing to do almost anything to alleviate or minimize the pain. Losing a loved one can cause us to consider any way we can avoid the current pain or the pain we are anticipating from loss. There are many ways we may try to **bargain**.[8]

  I **bargained** with myself, if I had understood the dream about the crowded church service, could I have prevented his death? If I had even shared the dream with someone who understands dreams, could we have asked God to block it? Or if Darryl had never taken the job at the convenience store in the first place, he would not have been there during the robbery. Could I or someone else have helped him to find a better job, one where his life wouldn't have been at risk?

- During our experience of processing grief (fourth stage), there comes a time when our imaginations calm down and we slowly start to look at the reality of our present situation. Bargaining no longer feels like an option, and we are faced with what is happening. Although this is a very natural stage of grief, dealing with **depression** after the loss of a loved one can be extremely isolating.[8]

  > I was so depressed to the extent that I stopped living and just existed; it hurt so bad to even think about it. I couldn't focus on school work, and my grades plummeted. My teachers tried to empathize with me when they saw that I was sinking into depression. My high school principal was also concerned for my well-being and made sure to check in on my family and me. My high school friends told me years after our high school graduation that I was a functioning zombie. Unfortunately, I didn't know at the time that I was operating in a serious state of **depression**.

- When we come to a place of **acceptance**, it is not that we no longer feel the pain of loss. However, we are no longer resisting the reality of our situation, and we are not struggling to make it something different. Sadness and regret can still be present in this phase, but the emotional survival tactics of denial, bargaining, and anger are less likely to be present.[8]

  > The final stage is **acceptance**. I don't know if after 39 years, if I have ever fully conquered this stage, which

leads me to believe that grief is definitely a process! To help me deal with this stage, I sometimes imagine how successful Darryl would have been (professionally, personally, spiritually, etc.), if he was still living. I've also imagined him as a husband, a father and an uncle to his nieces and nephews and have concluded that he would have excelled in each situation. In the early years after his death, I would dream about him frequently. In those dreams, he would come to me dressed sharp as when he was alive. He wouldn't talk but just step back to watch and protect me. These dreams were comforting to me and Darryl's way of letting me know that he was alright and that I would be alright too. Now, I try to live how God wants me to and to keep Darryl's memory alive.

I want to make sure that you understand that although the stages of grief are organized from the first to the fifth stage, you may or may not experience all of the stages. There is also the possibility that you will skip stages and/or not go in order from one to five. Don't feel pressured into thinking that you are not dealing with these stages correctly. Remember, every single person will grieve differently. Please do not measure yourself to others or allow people to compare your grief process to theirs or anyone else's. The most important thing for you to do is take time to heal. It is also crucial for you to seek professional mental help if you find that you are stuck in a certain stage for a long period of time or if you cannot function as you normally would.

Children and Grief

Let's face it, so many children have experienced the death of a loved one and it was very difficult for them to handle. Grief can be unbearable for an adult and even more so for children. Unfortunately, not enough attention is being brought to how death and grief affects children.

When a child experiences the death of a loved one, can it be classified as an Adverse Childhood Experience (ACEs)? My answer to this question is *yes*.

Of course, my personal ACE was experiencing my brother being murdered. Remember, this was a traumatic event that occurred when I was only fifteen years old. The state of my mental health was challenged with fear, paranoia and PTSD. My personal decision making was also tested in my young adult life.

There were times in my young adult years where I thought I had everything together by setting and making plans to accomplish certain goals, but then a curveball would be thrown at me. Some of those curveballs turned into roadblocks. The roadblocks came in the form of people entering my life trying to gain my trust. Too many times, I let my guard down and allowed people into my heart who didn't have a right to be there. They didn't have my best interest at heart. I realized that I was still traumatized and wasn't in a good headspace to say *no* to them. Unfortunately, they took up my mental space and forced me to make life choices that I wish I could change.

Common sense tells us that children will grow up to become adults. In knowing this, we must understand that childhood events or Adverse Childhood Experiences (ACEs) will have an impact on a child's future leading into adulthood (e.g., education, careers, creating their own family, etc.).

The Centers for Disease Control and Prevention website has vital information to help further explain ACEs. Let us take a look in detail at a few facts about ACEs and discuss possible ways to prevent them from happening.

"Adverse childhood experiences (ACEs) can have a tremendous impact on future violence victimization and perpetration, and lifelong health and opportunity."[3]

"ACEs are potentially traumatic events that occur in childhood (0-17 years)." Examples of traumatic events include, but are not limited to: a child experiencing abuse, neglect, violence, death of a family member (by suicide, murder, etc.) or a child could have witnessed violence with their own eyes. It is important to note that one's environment could have a negative impact on them, when problems such as substance abuse and mental health issues exist.[3]

Although ACEs are common, there are some things that can be done to help prevent them.

Here are *a few prevention strategies of ACEs from the CDC:*[3]

1. ***Strengthen economic supports to families***

   This can be accomplished by making sure the financial security of homes is secure

2. ***Promote social norms that protect against violence and adversity***

   Create educational campaigns and legislative approaches to reduce corporal punishment

3. ***Ensure a strong start for children***

   Establish high quality child care and encourage preschool enrichment with family engagement.

4. ***Teach skills***

   Social-emotional learning; parenting skills and family relationship approaches

5. ***Connect youth to caring adults and activities***

   Mentoring and after school programs

6. ***Intervene to lessen immediate and long-term harms***

   Victim centered services; Treatment to lessen the harms of ACEs; Treatment to prevent problem behavior and future involvement in violence; Family-centered treatment for substance use disorders

Statistics on Grief [2]

"Statistics on grief and loss show that a large part of the U.S. population grieves each year. While some mourn the loss of close friends or relatives, others face the loss of jobs, pets and relationships. Grief is a complex and painful experience unique to each individual, but nearly everyone goes through it."[2]

Grief Prevalence Facts [2]

- Older adults experience grief at a higher rate than younger adults or children. Spousal loss is common in older adults as well as the death of friends, siblings and cousins.
- About 2.5 million people die in the United States annually, each leaving an average of five grieving people behind.
- It's estimated that 1.5 million children (5% of children in the United States) have lost one or both parents by age 15.

Childhood Grief and Bereavement[2]

"Childhood grief is often a memorable experience, commonly marked by the death of a grandparent or older relative. Childhood grief statistics state that 1.5 million children live in a single-parent home because of the loss of one parent and nearly 2 million children under 18 have lost both parents.

The way grief in children is processed can be positively or negatively affected by others around them. Bereavement during childhood can also cause issues such as bedwetting, digestive problems and trouble sleeping."[2]

To help our children deal with loss, grief and bereavement, as adults, we must first come to grips with our own emotions. Now this may be easier said than done but, nevertheless, it is very important to do. When we do not own up to how a death affects us, then we could, in a sense, instruct a child to do the same thing. If a child sees that you are dismissing your feelings of grief by not talking about it or not showing any emotion, they will believe that is normal. This can, unfortunately, have negative long-term consequences such as not knowing how to deal with relationships and life, if death were to occur again. A fantasy world can be created which could become dangerous for anyone trying to exist in this "real" world.

Even though everyone grieves differently, there are commonalities in the bereavement process that we all share. To help children deal with their emotions about a death that directly impacts them, here are a few things to consider from this article: How to Help Children Deal with Loss | Psychology Today [5]

- As soon as possible, share with them that their loved one has passed away. It can become messy if they find out through someone else (i.e. from a non-relative or social media).

  > If my uncles had not decided to break the bad news to my sister and I, we could have easily heard about it on the news or from the neighbors. I cannot imagine how I would have reacted if that had been the case.

- Make sure that the one who shares this life changing information is someone that the child trusts and someone that they are familiar with.

  > If my mother was not traveling back home from out of state when this happened, I have no doubt that she would have been the one to inform us of our brother's death. However, my uncles were someone that we

trusted and they made sure that we were in an area we were comfortable in before telling us.

- Be truthful about what happened depending upon what they can handle and how the death occurred.

  Because of the nature of my brother's death, I was not informed of every detail of how he died. I was only given general information. It was not until the actual murder trial took place that I found out more specific details.

- Be honest with your child about the feelings that they may encounter in the days ahead. There may be times that they will experience sadness, confusion, fear, denial or any of the stages of grief. Experiencing none, all or some of these feelings does not mean that it is a bad thing or that something is wrong with them.

  I experienced a lot of fear, PTSD, and confusion because I did not want it to be true. I did not want to talk about it because then I would have to come to the realization that it was true.

Understanding PTSD: Trauma impacts everyone differently, depending on the nature of the trauma, presence or lack of social supports, participation in treatment, and coping mechanisms.[7]

- Many individuals who experience traumatic events will have temporary difficulty adjusting and coping with the trauma, but it should get better with time and self-care. It is extremely important to make your own health a priority.[7]

- PTSD can significantly strain the emotional and mental health of friends and loved ones. If you know someone that is suffering from PTSD, understand that avoidance and withdrawal are part of the process. Please make yourself available to listen. You may also suggest that they seek help from a mental health professional[7]

- Take time to explain how the family will lay the loved one to rest. Tell them what will take place at the funeral, burial, etc. and allow them to ask questions if they do not understand.

> I was so young and my mind could not easily process my brother no longer being alive, so I could not think straight during the funeral. I became hysterical when a recording of my brother's voice was played as a tribute to his memory. I wonder if my reaction would have been different if I had known that his voice recording was going to be played.

- Keep the deceased's memory alive so the child will not forget them. You can do this by having pictures and videos accessible. Allow the child to set up a time when they want to sit down and reminisce. This can be done on a special occasion, such as the decedent's birthday. Or maybe they would like to plant a tree in their loved one's memory. If the loved one died from a disease such as cancer or diabetes, encourage them to find creative ways to make contributions to help find a cure. Also, if the deceased had a particular hobby or career that was of interest to the child, maybe they can continue in it as their own hobby or career.

> In this world of social media, I love to post pictures and videos of my late brother on certain anniversary days, such as his birthdate and on the date of his death. This helps me to keep his memory alive in my mind. It actually helps to open a dialogue with others who never knew him about who he was. I also found myself continuing in his career as a radio broadcaster. I am doing what he loved to do and it has been life changing for me.

- Be very attentive to a child's behavior if the family dynamic has changed after a loved one passes away. Whether the number of family members decreased by one or more than one, the child sees it as a major change in their own life. Everyone else may be still alive (mother, father, sister), but that one person is no longer in the same house or easily accessible to talk to or interact with. It will take time to adjust and get used to a new normal without them being around.

> Before my brother died, all five of us lived at home (mom, my two sisters and my brother). After he died, both of my sisters moved out (one became married and the other went off to college), so it was just me at home with my mom. As the youngest child, that was rough for me, and truth be told, I was angry about that. I was angry for two reasons: 1) my family dynamic changed so quickly from five to two people at home, starting with

my brother's demise and 2) I knew things would not go back the way they were as much as I wanted them to!

Remember, all of these tips are very important in order to avoid stress, mental health challenges, etc. I always say that it is crucial to express yourself and not keep things bottled up inside. Doing so will hinder your ability to manage stress. I strongly encourage and advocate therapy and/or counseling sessions. It is NEVER too late to seek counseling. If you feel like you, your child or someone you love needs further assistance dealing with grief and death, I implore you to contact a mental health professional.

At the time of the writing of this book, we will observe thirty-nine years (August, 2022) since the passing of my brother. When I began writing this book, it obviously brought up memories that I had not addressed in years, I actually re-lived the tragedy and it was very unpleasant. I found myself viewing everything from my fifteen-year-old eyes again, including the details of my brother's death. And of course, I cried like a baby throughout this project. Yes, I would cry and then stop writing to get myself together or write while crying.

During one of these breakdowns, my husband asked me, "Do you think you need counseling?" I immediately responded and said that I would definitely consider it once my book was completed. But his question stayed on my mind and it made me think, 'why not consult a therapist?' Anyone who knows me, understands that my mission and aim is to help others and if that means referring them to a therapist, I will do just that. I have professional counselors and therapists on speed dial as referrals to those who are in need and many have benefitted from their services. But what about me?

I endured something horrible as a child and never experienced a counseling or therapy session to help deal with it. Back then, I do not remember it being suggested to any of us. If I am being completely honest, I do not know if I would have been open to it anyway. Therapy and counseling in the Black community has a history of not being well received, especially in the early 1980s. However, if I knew then what I know now, I would have run to the first licensed professional counselor's office that I saw!

*****

With all that being said, I am proud to announce that after being confronted with that question from my husband, I picked up the phone the next day and contacted the same counselor that I normally recommend to others and made an appointment to begin my therapy sessions!

Yes, I know it has been almost four decades since that tragedy, but I realized that this is something that I need to do. So, while I am creating a masterpiece to help others cope with death and grief, I am finally being ministered to professionally on how to cope with my own personal grief. My LPC is helping me to hear my *"heartbeat"*again!

PART 3 - REBUILD, REFOCUS, LIVE!!

CHAPTER 7

I Hear A Heartbeat

Bereavement Chairperson

Nine years after my brother passed away, I became a part of the Bereavement Committee at my church. As of January, 2022, I have worked in this department for thirty years. I currently work in the position of Bereavement Committee Chairperson.

The purpose of this committee is to assist families during their time of bereavement. If a member of the congregation loses a loved one, we do not ever want them to feel alone. Although death is a part of life, it can be difficult to navigate through the process when you are personally touched by it. My late pastor used to have a saying, "We do not want anyone to fall through the cracks." He simply meant that even though everyone grieves differently, do not let them grieve alone or allow them to think they have to grieve alone.

As the Bereavement Committee Chairperson, my duties are similar to an air traffic controller. When families need my services, I step in to assess what their needs are by coordinating an orderly flow of tasks in order to create a well-planned funeral service for their loved one. Sometimes when I sit down with families, I am able to minister to them by hand-holding them through every step or sharing with them what to expect in the days ahead after the funeral. When they are in need of mental health care, I will refer them to a mental health care professional.

What a far cry from the young fifteen year old, who thirty-nine years ago could not even sit through the entire funeral service of my brother because of the hurt, confusion and fear that gripped me. Ironic, huh? I absolutely never would have thought that I would be serving in this position as an adult! I didn't think that I would ever be able to go on with life and deal with losing Darryl!

Well, as you can see God has a plan, a purpose and definitely a sense of humor. The truth is that I believe God allowed me to experience grief in that horrible way so that I can empathize and sympathize with all the individuals that I have helped down through the years. I always say that our personal journey is not for us alone, it is meant to be an example to help someone else become victorious through a similar situation. You see, our God has great love and an innumerable amount of tender mercy for each and every human being. **"You intended to harm me, but God intended it all for good. He brought me to this position so I could save the lives of many people." Genesis 50:20 NLT**

Psychology Major

When I initially began college in 1985, I wasn't too sure of what I wanted to study or do in life. I was still adjusting to a new normal and it was rough. I took a lot of general classes with a few that were focused on sociology. Honestly, I didn't know what career I wanted to pursue; I just knew that I wanted to help people. I wasn't able to correctly focus on being a college student, not to mention, the cost of college was overwhelming for my family to handle during that time. Unfortunately, those were the reasons behind me not continuing on and I eventually left school.

In 2009, I returned back to college to finish what I started, or so I thought. I transferred to a different college and it was the best decision I could have ever made! After being introduced to a phenomenal advisor who shared my same passions, I became a psychology major. I took classes part-time and worked part-time. I learned so much about myself and humanity through the area of psychology. It is also here where I learned to understand in the natural how to deal with death/grief. This was indeed a fulfilling journey coupled with life changes and personal challenges, but I was able to walk across the stage in 2013. My overall plan is to return to take a few more classes and obtain my Masters in Psychology. My ultimate goal is to become a licensed professional counselor, LPC.

Radio Broadcast Host/Podcast Host

In 2013, I was bitten by the radio show host bug. On November 27, the first session of "Mind, Body and Soul w/ANet" aired. I initially aired on a terrestrial AM radio station weekly for 30 minutes.

This radio show was created as a connection between psychology and the Bible to help the many people who are hurting across our nation. Our main concern is making sure that mental health issues are psychologically and spiritually addressed and not ignored.

I accomplish this by providing a safe space for listeners to vent, ask questions and get answers about any mental health situations. For this reason, I have addressed this platform as "sessions," instead of episodes or shows. To date, my guests have included licensed professional therapists, mental health professionals, psychologists, authors, religious leaders, actors, directors, photographers, and many others.

"Mind, Body and Soul w/ANet" became a huge hit because as many have said this type of show was rare yet very much needed. Within 2 years, we went from airing for 30 minutes weekly to airing two hours on a weekly basis. In November of 2023, we will celebrate ten years of quality radio programming.

In November 2018, "Mind, Body and Soul w/ANet" collaborated with the leader of Sakal the Center, Chicago and created another radio show, entitled, "Mind, Body and Soul: AnD Conversation." This additional radio show joined two wonderful hosts together to dialogue about everyday conversations. We tackle topics from a psychological and spiritual perspective in a judgment free zone.

MindMending in the Net Podcast

In 2020, I was encouraged by a millennial to begin my own podcast show to reach other audiences. This encouragement came from one of my beautiful nieces who is Chief Content Officer and host of her own award-winning podcast show. Well, I had to learn to move with the times and connect with other generations. As a result, "Mind-Mending in the Net" podcast was born on May 31, 2021!

This podcast experience was created as a NET for the mind to mend in! I was inspired to make sure positive mental health was the focus of the podcast. Why? Well, by that time, the world had been on lockdown for about a year and many did not know how to quiet that little voice in our heads that was getting louder and louder. That voice was sometimes screaming, HELP!

I simply provide an opportunity where anyone can find WHAT mental health means, realize WHEN it's important to address and when those issues occur, know WHERE mental health resources are available and understand HOW we can develop POSITIVE mental health. The purpose of this podcast is to give a safe space and provide the tools for you, the listener, to mend your mind!

Remember, I told you that my mantra is, "Everything starts in the mind," and I utilize it extensively on this podcast.

I never imagined that I would become a radio show host or a podcast host. I never even planned to make a career out of it. Yet, here I am almost four decades after my brother's death, walking in the same vocation that he started in. It is truly an honor and privilege to serve in this area and to keep his dream alive.

Positive Mental Health Ambassador

In 2020, in the midst of the Covid-19 pandemic, the Lord placed it upon my heart to further my psychology background by taking classes to become a Positive Mental Health Ambassador. It became evident to me that during this unprecedented time that the entire world was facing the fact that mental health is being challenged every day. The absence of mental health is very serious and it not only affects one particular individual but everyone they will come in contact with (family, friends, co-workers, loved ones, etc.).

The purpose of a PMHA is to help people struggling with mental health and to promote better mental health in our society. In this capacity, I do not provide treatment, I leave that to the mental health professionals. However, I can stand up and encourage discussions about taboo conversations or tackle the big elephant in the room. Because of my strong desire to help people, I have the training to speak up when anyone finds themselves struggling mentally.

To help you, your child and/or your loved one deal with grief, I would like to share with you the **REAL-SF** system.[6]

It is a simple framework with six steps that can be used in almost any situation.

1. **Recognize** with someone who is having a mental health crisis

    This may be difficult to accomplish because many people hide mental issues well. Pay extra attention to your child if their behavior changes from a regular routine. Are their grades dropping, have their interests in their favorite hobbies, recreational activities or sports diminished?

2. **Engage** people in a friendly and non-threatening manner

    The goal is to get them communicating. Are they adjusting well or struggling to adjust after experiencing death? Let them know that they can confide in you (or a professional) exactly what they are feeling.

3. **Assist** if there is an acute crisis happening at the time

    This step is important to carry out if you need to make an immediate intervention in situations, such as if someone is having a panic attack, unconscious or badly injured.

4. **Listen** to them and give them a friendly ear to talk through problems

    The art of listening is crucial but is not easy to accomplish. You want your child to know that you will not interrupt them when they express themselves. However, sharing private feelings with family members still may not come easily. In these cases, a professional therapist or counselor could be recommended. Either way, the big picture of having someone to listen is therapeutic and must be in full view.

5. **Signpost** them to professional help, where appropriate

    Know your limitations! Licensed professional counselors, family therapists, emergency (911) service personnel, crisis centers, etc., are examples of trained professionals that you may need to call upon. If you have NOT been trained in these areas, **please** do NOT take it upon yourself to treat your child (or anyone else) if they are in need of these services.

6. **Follow-up** with them at a later point

    This is the last step which is also the most forgotten step. Depending on the situation, if you dealt with your child directly or referred them to a professional, you are probably just relieved that you got them the help they needed. But please make it a priority to check on them periodically. Be strategic, not annoying when following up with them. Remember, mental health problems don't magically go away and making an intervention isn't a one-time thing.

Small Business Owner

I am the CEO of GetcaughtinANet Incorporated. This company was legalized in 2021 and it is the umbrella for both my radio and podcast shows. My mission, my drive and my concern are to do whatever I can to help people and my company affords me that opportunity.

There are so many heartbeats
yet to be heard

Many of us are in a tug of war mentally, sometimes on a daily basis. The pressures of life will test whether we have the peace of God or just a piece of God.

Anything from trials, tests, tragic situations, death of a loved one, loss of a job and so much more will tend to trigger mental illness (depression, bi-polar disorder, schizophrenia, anxiety, panic disorders, PTSD, psychosis, panic attacks, etc.). Be realistic, these situations can happen at any time, so what are you going to do about it?

I encourage you to grab THE PEACE of God and not just a PIECE of God!!

Be careful for nothing; but in everything by prayer and supplication with thanksgiving let your requests be made known unto God. And the peace of God, which passeth all understanding, shall keep your hearts and minds through Christ Jesus. Finally, brethren, whatsoever things are true, whatsoever things are honest, whatsoever things are just, whatsoever things are pure, whatsoever things are lovely, whatsoever things are of good report; if there be any virtue, and if there be any praise, think on these things. Philippians 4:6-8

I can't help but smile
I can't help but to look out in the {literary} audience
And see you smiling back at me
Because right now
I hear your heartbeat

ABOUT THE AUTHOR

Annette Harris, is multifaceted, and as the CEO of her own corporation, a broadcast and podcast host, and a Certified Mental Health Ambassador she absolutely loves all things "psychology"! Annette has been known to analyze everything and everyone, because she gets satisfaction out of understanding what is really going on in an individual's mind. Reading, writing, watching intense television dramas and suspense filled movies, listening to thought provoking podcasts, singing, going to concerts, taking walks to enjoy nature, eating good food, going on vacation and online shopping are some of the things she does to maintain positive mental health. Annette's  immediate and extended family are extremely important to her and spending time with her siblings, her nieces and nephews is essential to making lasting memories. In September, 2022, Annette and her husband, Anthony Harris, will celebrate 25 wonderful years of marriage.

BIBLIOGRAPHY

1 https://greatergood.berkeley.edu/topic/forgiveness/definition

2 Grief By The Numbers: Facts and Statistics - The Recovery Village Drug and Alcohol Rehab

3 Adverse Childhood Experiences (ACEs) (cdc.gov)

4 Over 5 million children have lost a parent or caregiver to COVID, study finds: Live COVID updates (msn.com)

5 How to Help Children Deal with Loss | Psychology Today

6 Mental Health Ambassador Course Notes – Udemy Online Course

7 MindSpring Mental Health Alliance (mindspringhealth.org) – Understanding PTSD Seminar

8 The Five Stages of Grief www.verywellmind.com

9 Elisabeth Kübler-Ross - PMC www.nih.gov

www.ingramcontent.com/pod-product-compliance
Lightning Source LLC
Chambersburg PA
CBHW071019120626
46546CB00003B/1163